HANG GLIDING & PARAGLIDING

Noel Whittall started flying in 1973 with a home-built hang glider. He went on to become Chairman of the British Hang Gliding Association and later, Secretary of CIVL, the Hang Gliding and Paragliding Commission of the FAI, a post he held until 2001.

His hang gliding has taked Noel all over Britain and to Europe and the USA, participating in the growing sport and photographing it from the early days. Noel has written several books about the different aspects of it. He is based in the north of England but travels extensively in Europe, flying for his own delight or officiating at international competitions.

These days Noel says that he is best known for being the father of Rob Whittall, the first pilot to win World Championships in both Hang Gliding and Paragliding!

Copyright © ticktock Entertainment Ltd 2008

First published in Great Britain in 2008 by ticktock Media Ltd,
2 Orchard Business Centre, North Farm Road, Tunbridge Wells, Kent, TN2 3XF

ticktock project editor: Julia Adams
ticktock project designer: Sara Greasley
ticktock picture researcher: Lizzie Knowles

With thanks to: David Wootton, Diana LeCore, Anna Brett

ISBN 978 1 84696 527 2 pbk

Printed in China

Picture credits (t=top; b=bottom; c=centre; l=left; r=right):
Age Fotostock/Superstock: 56b. David Bagley/ Alamy: 34/35. Denis Balibouse: 48/49t, 58. Denis Balibouse/ Red Bull Photofiles: 24/25, 44/45, 48b. Bettmann/ Corbis: 10/11t. Elizabeth Czitronyi/ Alamy: 57t. Steve Elkins: 19b. Flybubble Paragliding School, www.flybubble.co.uk: 29t. Getty Images: 9t, 9b. Ulrich Grill/ Red Bull Photofiles: 31tr. John Heiney: 59b. INSADCO Photography/ Alamy: 42t. Vitek Ludvik/ Red Bull Photofiles: 28. Alfredo Martinez/ Red Bull Photofiles: 20/21. Mary Evans Picture llbrary: 7c. Ian Mills, 10fifty.com: 15tr. Paraglidingshop.co.uk: 33t. Christian Pondella/ Red Bull Photofiles: 49b. Francois Portmann/ Red Bull Photofiles: 51c. Bill Ross/ Corbis: 29b. Pasi Salminen/ Red Bull Photofiles: 51tr. Shutterstock: 1, 3, 4/5, 12/13, 14t, 15cl, 16, 17t, 17b, 20b, 22, 23bl x3, 27 all, 32, 43tr, 61. Bernhard Spöttel/ Red Bull Photofiles: 46. Square1.com: 33br. The Print Collector/ Alamy: 8. Noel Whittall: 2, 10b, 11b, 18/19, 26, 37b, 38, 39t, 39b, 40/41t, 40b, 41b, 43bl, 47t, 47b, 50t, 53br, 57c, 59t, 60. Wikipedia: 36/37t. Wingsofrogallo.org: 23tr. David Wootton: 6/7t, 17c, 30t, 33c, 52cr, 52/53t, 54/55. Tim Wright/ Corbis: 36b.

Every effort has been made to trace copyright holders, and we apologise in advance for any omissions. We would be pleased to insert the appropriate acknowledgments in any subsequent edition of this publication.

Contents

HANG GLIDING & PARAGLIDING

Gliding is arguably one of the most extreme sports out there. It provides what many say is the ultimate rush. Running off a cliff and feeling the wind pick up your glider is an experience that is unmatched by any other.

The earliest recorded attempt at flying was made in China and dates back to 559. For hundreds of years flying remained a dream, although many people were injured and even killed trying.

There were many attempts to perform unpowered flight – some tried to make flapping wings to imitate birds' flight, but they lacked the power to flap them. Some tied themselves to kites but couldn't control them. Then, in the 19th century, experimenters studied the flight of gliding birds like the albatross. These birds rarely need to flap their wings. The secrets of flying began to be unlocked by people such as Otto Lilienthal and Octave Chanute.

HANG GLIDING & PARAGLIDING

Hang gliders and paragliders are completely unpowered – they fly in the same way as gliding birds do

An early attempt at flying – Le Besnier of Sable, France, managed to cross a river with his flapping paddles after launching from a height (1678)

Modern hang gliding started in the 1960s, when the right combination of material and knowledge came together. People were able to create simple gliders that could be launched on foot. Paragliders followed in the 1980s.

The main difference between paragliders and hang glider is that hang gliders have wings have a stiff framework, whereas paragliders are completely soft, just like parachutes.

They are both so light that they are easily carried by one person.

The French name for these sports is 'le vol libre'. The English translation is 'free flight', and that is just what it is all about: flying free, without an engine and without noise, leaving no marks on the countryside.

Hang gliding pioneer Otto Lilienthal undertook many test flights and endured many an injury while developing the first hang glider

Otto Lilienthal, Germany

The first great hang glider pilot was Otto Lilienthal. He was a German inventor who made wings out of wood and canvas in the 1880s. Otto hung by his armpits in his glider and gained some control by swinging his legs, but it was not always enough. Otto died of a fractured spine in a glider crash in 1893 – five years after he began flying. By then, he had made about 2,000 flights. His studies inspired the invention of the powered aeroplane, a few years later.

Chanute's assistant, Augustus Moore Herring, flying the biplane glider

Octave Chanute, USA

American Octave Chanute made a fortune as an engineer, designing railways and stockyards. Like many before him he dreamed of flight. He built a biplane glider which his assistant tested on sand dunes at the shore of Lake Michigan, near Chicago, in 1896. The pilot hung by the armpits – just like Lilienthal – so control of the glider was difficult.

9

After three years of experimenting with large gliders, the Wright brothers built and flew the world's first successful powered aircraft in 1903.

A very early Rogallo glider prepares for take-off

In the 1950s, American scientist Dr. Francis Rogallo was working in the space industry developing parachutes for spacecraft. His ideas would be adapted by sporting fliers to form the shape which everyone now recognises as a hang glider. These were often called 'Rogallos'.

The modern hang glider was invented by John Dickenson in Australia in 1963. He used the Rogallo wing shape and added a swing seat so that all the pilot's body weight could be used for control. The first ones were towed into the air behind boats at water-ski exhibitions

HANG GLIDING & PARAGLIDING

Wilbur Wright watches Orville Wright pilot the first successful flight
in the Wright Flyer at Kitty Hawk, North Carolina, USA, in 1903

The paraglider

An early ram-air parachute

From time-to-time people tried gliding with parachutes, but true success with this did not come until 1978. A group of Frenchmen began flying a new invention, ram-air parachutes, from steep mountains near Mieussy, in the French Alps. Their original idea was to practice for parachuting competitions without the cost of hiring an aeroplane to jump from. But flying from mountains was thrilling and fun! Soon manufacturers started making more efficient canopies designed specifically for gliding and the paraglider was born.

Ram-air Aerofoil canopy which is sub-divided into separate cells. The entire canopy is open at the front and closed at the back so it is literally rammed full of air and becomes a solid flying wing.

chapter 2: the basics

Hang gliders are usually launched by running off a hill or mountain. They can also be towed into the air using a microlight tug aircraft. They can soon by flying at heights of up to 15,000 feet.

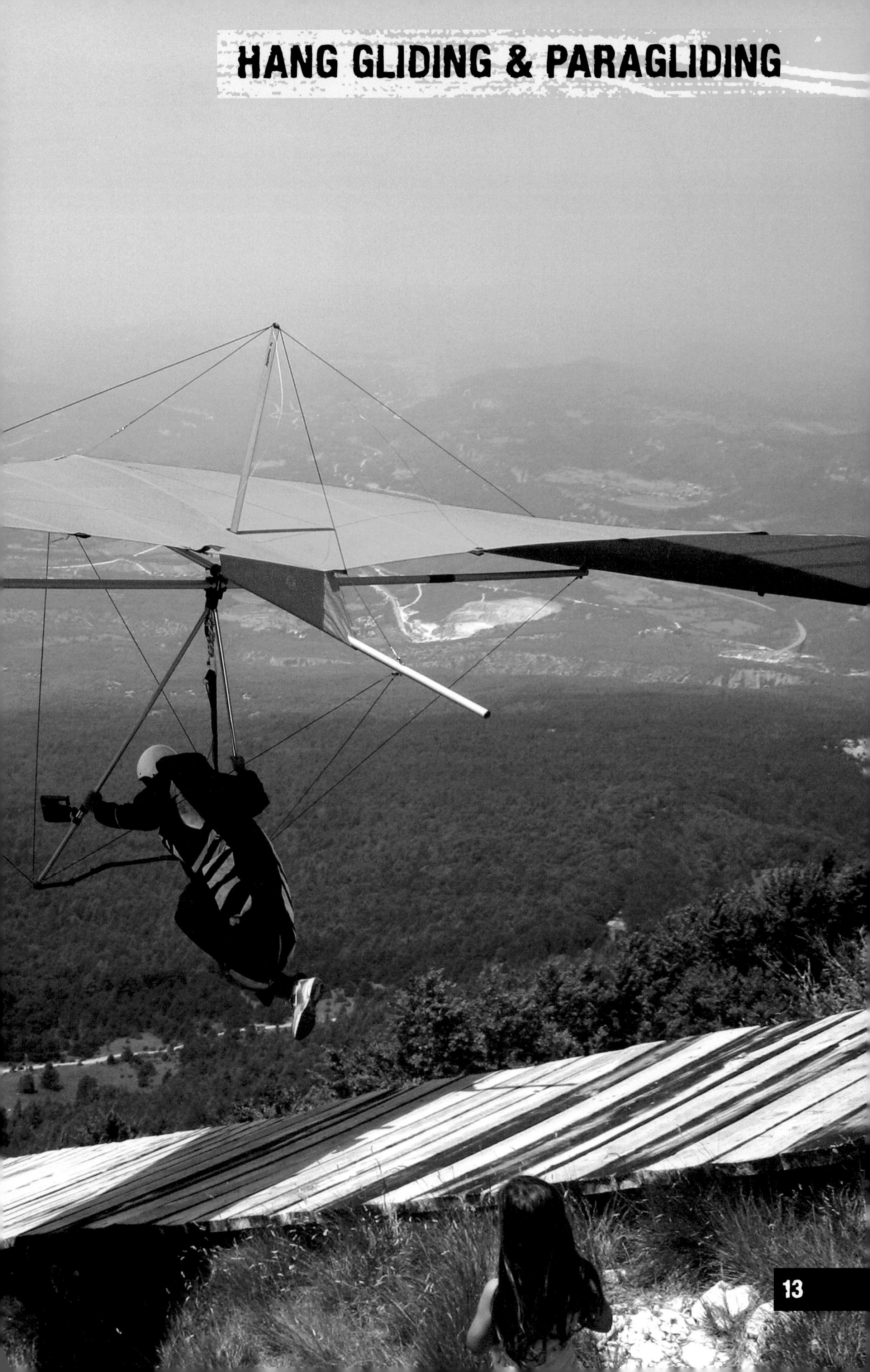

leading edge

Gliders can fly for hours without a motor because they seek out rising air. In still air, a glider will sink due to the pull of gravity. When gliders find rising air, also called lift, it counteracts the gravity and the glider will stay airborne.

The large wing of a glider generates the lift it needs to fly by keeping the front edge (the leading edge) tilted up higher than the back (the trailing edge) as it moves forwards. This causes air to be deflected downwards and the wing reacts by trying to rise. Gliders don't have engines to push them forwards.

trailing edge

Staying up

A glider keeps the air passing over its wings at just the right speed by going downhill all the time, like freewheeling on a bike. If you see a hang glider or paraglider climbing upwards, it is because the air in that part of the sky is moving upwards faster than gravity is making the glider sink.

There are three types of natural lift:

Ridge lift: When wind meets a ridge or hill it is forced upwards. Pilots try to launch into this ridge lift as it will help them to climb immediately. Ridge lift rarely goes more than twice the height of the ridge.

Thermal lift: Thermals are patches of air which have been made extra warm by the sun. Hot air rises and thermals are often powerful enough to take gliders up to the clouds.

Wave lift: This is similar to ridge lift, but goes much higher. It happens when wind flows down the back of one hill and is 'bounced' up again when it meets the front of the next one. This can give smooth powerful lift which may go thousands of feet into the sky.

All aircraft, from hang gliders to jumbo jets, use three basic control movements: roll, pitch and yaw. On most hang gliders, pilots do this by swinging their bodies. This is called weight-shift control.

Roll

Roll means tilting one wing lower than the other. This is done by the pilot shifting their body sideways. This automatically causes a turn in the direction of the lower wing.

Pitch

Pitch means tilting the front of the glider up or down. This controls the airspeed. Pulling the body forwards lowers the front, making the glider speed up. Push back, and it slows down.

Yaw

Yaw is when one side of the glider is moved forwards, causing the glider to turn. When the right-hand side of the glider is moved forwards, the glider moves to the left. In hang gliding yaw is far less important than in paragliding, as rolling is a far more effective way of turning this type of glider.

This paraglider is taking a left-hand turn by bringing forward the right-hand side of the canopy

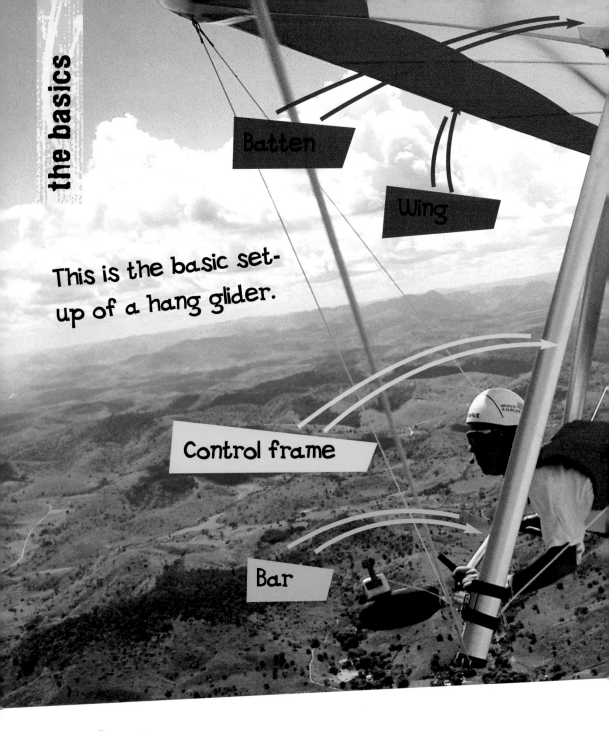

Batten

Wing

This is the basic set-up of a hang glider.

Control frame

Bar

The **wing** material fits over the main frame. The material is called the sail. It is made from heavy-grade nylon or Dacron. Several ribs, called **battens**, fit into long pockets sewn into each side to keep it in the correct aerofoil shape.

The **control frame** is connected to the **keel** close to the hang point. It is made from aluminium, but is much thinner than the keel. It is joined to the main frame with steel wires.

Hang point

Carabiner

Keel

Harness

The **hang-point** is a strong webbing loop on the keel at the centre of the control frame.

The **harness** joins to the hang point with a **carabiner**. The carabiner carries all the pilot's weight, so it has to be very strong. Harnesses are designed so that the pilot can stand up for take-offs and landings, and lie flat during flight.

Quick-release catches make the glider easy to assemble for flight. The glider can be folded into a roll that can be carried on a car roof.

Red Bull

www.intellisite.ch
the new generation of websites

Unlike hang gliders, paragliders have no stiff framework. The entire shape of the wing depends on being inflated with the air it passes through. This is called the ram-air effect. Paraglider wings are usually called canopies.

Canopy

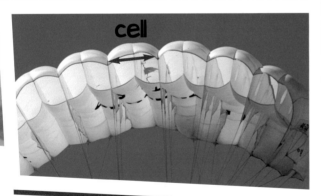

cell

The **canopy** material is light nylon which is airtight. It is built up from a large number of cells which are sewn together side-by side. Each cell is open at the front which allows it to fill with air as the canopy flies along.

The pilot sits in a **harness** which is joined to the canopy by many lines. These are carefully positioned so that when the canopy takes the weight of the pilot it remains in the perfect shape to provide lift.

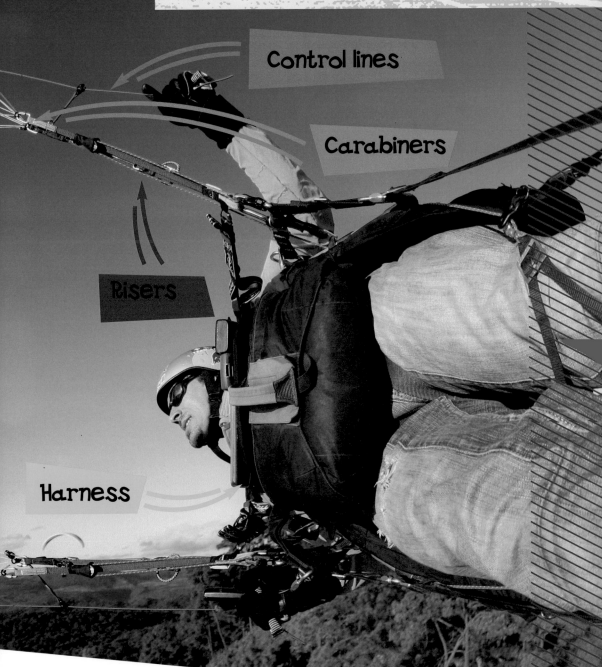

Control lines

Carabiners

Risers

Harness

The lines group together close to the pilot and are joined to short strips of webbing called **risers**. These risers link to the harness with small **carabiners**.

As well as the lines which suspend the pilot, there is an extra pair which run from the trailing edge of each side of the canopy to handles in front of the risers. These are the **control lines**, usually referred to as brakes. The brakes can be used individually and help the pilot yaw the canopy.

21

Paragliders fly more slowly than hang gliders. Controlling a paraglider in the air is very simple. To cruise, the brake handles are held about level with the pilot's shoulders – this gives the trim speed. Raising both handles upwards increases speed slightly, and pulling them both down reduces it.

Hang glider pilots use their weight to control the glider by shifting it to the side they wish to steer towards. Apart from the steering, both types of glider are very challenging to handle. It takes a lot of training to control them. Launching and landing can be especially tricky.

A paraglider demonstrating a roll; some display pilots use smoke flares to mark their movements in the sky

Trim speed Speed the glider flies at if the pilot is not putting any effort into the controls

Landing

Landing a hang glider needs careful timing. The pilot first slows the wing by gently pushing the bar out. Next, they move their hands to the sides of the control frame to slow it down as it reaches the ground.

Launching

The most tricky part of paragliding is launching. If you watch skilled pilots, you will see that they first get the wing arranged neatly on the ground. Then they pull on some of the lines to let air into the cells which starts shaping the wing. Next, they pull both the risers evenly so the wing rises above them like a giant kite. They don't start the short run into the wind to take-off until the canopy is overhead and they have checked that it is fully inflated.

chapter 3: the gear

Gliding sports are dangerous, and sometimes accidents cannot be avoided. But with the right gear, pilots can limit the danger. It is essential pilots have the correct equipment to help them cope with the fickle conditions of the sky.

Hang glider and paraglider pilots need to dress to suit high altitude conditions. Even though it may be warm on the ground, once they are flying they will be going through the air at speeds of up to 145 kilometres per hour, so they will feel a constant wind-chill effect.

High climbers

Hangliders and paragliders may also climb high – as high as the clouds on a good day. The higher they go, the colder the air becomes. Gliders can reach 15,000 feet. At this height, temperatures are an average of -17°C.

Helmet

A helmet is a must. Head injuries can be life-threatening, and it is easy to misjudge a landing on rough ground. For high flights a balaclava is worn under the helmet. Competition pilots wear streamlined helmets to reduce drag (see image left).

Goggles

Close-fitting sun glasses or goggles are essential because eye-damaging UV rays in sunlight are much stronger at high altitude. Pilots choose types which make the clouds more visible. Often these have orange lenses.

Flying suit

A one-piece flying suit is often worn for paragliding. Hang glider pilots, who fly in warm streamlined harnesses with only their heads and shoulders sticking out, often just wear jeans and windproof jackets.

Pilots are exposed to particularly tough conditions: closeness to the Sun, extremely low temperatures and high winds. This calls for some additional equipment to make the flight as safe and successful as possible.

Speed arms

Anything flapping in the high winds makes for extra drag, so the glider cannot fly as well. When speed is of the essence, pilots wear elastic Lycra sleeves over their flying suits to keep the drag from their bodies to a minimum.

Warm hands and feet

Keeping the hands and feet warm on a long, high flight is a problem for paraglider pilots. Ski gloves or mitts are usually worn for all-weather flying. Even on really warm days, pilots will wear thin leather gloves for hand protection. Without them, it is easy to damage your fingers on the control lines. Hang glider pilots have less of a problem. Some wear thick gloves, but many prefer mitts which are fitted to the control bar. Feet need to be protected by good boots, so paragliders wear specially designed lightweight boots giving lots of ankle support.

Sun protection

Even if the air feels cool on top of a mountain, or when high up on a glider, the sun can burn you easily. The dangerous UV rays in sunlight are much stronger at the heights gliders scale. Aside from protecting the eyes, it is essential to use strong sunscreen to avoid severe sunburns.

In order to avoid ending up lost or over dangerous terrain, glider pilots carry a large amount of gadgets and instruments with them.

Altimeter, variometer and GPS

In a hang glider, the control frame functions as the pilot's cockpit. The pilot lies in the harness and has the instruments mounted on the control frame where they are easy to see. Paraglider pilots have the instruments fitted into a waist-pack which is clipped to the harness and rests on their thighs in flight.

Altimeter/Vario/GPS A few years ago all these instruments were separate, but now it is usual for the altimeter, vario and GPS to be combined into a single small case not much bigger than a mobile phone.

GPS

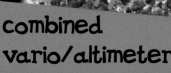

combined
vario/altimeter

A paraglider's cockpit is
attached to their harness

This is a list of equipment a pilot will take on a flight:

Altimeter, to show the height the glider is currently flying at.

Variometer (usually called just 'vario') to show how fast the glider is climbing or sinking. It can be dangerous to rise too quickly and too high, as oxygen levels decrease at high altitude. Pilots can pass out before they realise they are in danger. They need oxygen equipment if they are going to fly above 12,000 feet.

GPS to show and record the glider's route.

Two-way radio in case the pilot is in danger and needs to send out an emergency signal.

As well as the instruments, there will be a holder for a special map which shows airports and routes called 'airways'. These 'sky roads' are reserved for airliners and other powered planes.
It is important that hang glider and paraglider pilots keep clear of these parts of the sky.

Exposure to the weather and unpredictable thermals and wind currents have led to many accidents for gliders. Because there are some conditions that a pilot cannot control, most carry a rescue parachute fitted to their harness.

The rescue chute is joined to the glider by a strong line called a strop. The glider and the pilot come down together under the rescue chute. There is no way of steering, so rescue chutes are only ever used in a real emergency such as a mid-air collision, or a collapsed canopy.

When the canopy of a paraglider collapses and becomes badly tangled, there is no way of landing safely without a rescue parachute

Landing protection

Landings can go wrong. For example, if a paraglider pilot tries to land in rough air or needs to touch down on dangerous terrain. To protect the pilot, the harnesses have built-in safety features. This can be a thick layer of plastic foam fitted down the back and under the seat of the harness to protect the pilot's spine.

The spine protection is built into the back part

A paragliding harness with an in-built airbag and extra spine protection

Whatever type of protection is fitted, glider pilots are taught to keep their feet together and knees bent, as the landing impact can cause serious injuries.

In woodland areas, glider pilots carry a long cord in their harness to help them climb down if they land in a tree! They also carry a special knife to cut away the reserve parachute if they land in high wind and are dragged by it.

Some pilots use special knives that have protected blades so they don't injure themselves

chapter 4: gliders

Both hang gliders and paragliders have come a long way since manufacturers started producing them for sport in the 1970s. Today, there are types of gliders that cater to the needs of competition professionals and beginners alike.

Training gliders have fairly loose sails, so they fly slowly and are much easier to handle than competition ones. Students on their early flights are kept close to the ground by instructors using rope tethers. Once they are used to the feel of the glider, the ropes are removed and solo flight begins.

The most basic distinction within hang gliders is between training and competition gliders. Both are controlled in exactly the same way, but competition gliders are designed to have a higher top speed. All parts of a competition glider and its pilot are streamlined. The glider's frame is very stiff, to hold the sail taut so that it stays in shape at speeds of up to 145 km/h..

Hang gliders don't always fly off hills; here is a competition glider being tow-launched behind a microlight tug

In competitions, the usual aim is to fly a route across country as quickly as possible. The route may be 160 kilometres or more. Pilots have to find lots of areas of rising air (lift) to take them along the course. Unfortunately, there is always sink between patches of lift.

The fast glide is good when flying from one area of lift to another — pilots need to be in sinking air for as little time as possible. A very stiff wing is fastest, but difficult to turn by weight-shift, so there is a cord which the pilots can use to slacken it a little.

The stiffer the wing, the faster the glider, but only experienced pilots can control a sophisticated competition hang glider

The Swift

The Swift is a type of hang glider that is very closely related to a sailplane. The performance of a Swift is spectacular compared to ordinary hang gliders: it can be flown slowly enough to take off and land at running speed, yet has a top speed in the air of about 120 km/h. At its most efficient gliding speed, it sinks only one foot for every twenty-six that it flies forward. That's about twice as good as an average hang glider and three times as good as a paraglider. The Swift achieves this by having extremely stiff wings and extra movable flaps on the wings to steer it, like a plane.

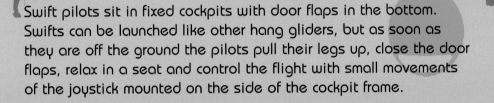

Swift pilots sit in fixed cockpits with door flaps in the bottom. Swifts can be launched like other hang gliders, but as soon as they are off the ground the pilots pull their legs up, close the door flaps, relax in a seat and control the flight with small movements of the joystick mounted on the side of the cockpit frame.

Swifts perform better than almost any other hang gliders but are not as easy to carry about. The wings can be removed, but are rigid and cannot be rolled up for storage. A Swift will fit in a big box on top of a car, but two people are needed to put the glider together and prepare it for launch. Because of this, Swifts are rather rare, so you will be lucky if you spot one.

Spoilers

Rigids

A new type of hang glider came along in the
early 1990s called a rigid. Instead of using an aluminium
frame, these gliders get their strength from a carbon fibre frame.
The wings are rigid and use moveable surfaces to make them turn.

Pilots of rigids hang in the same type of harness as normal hang gliders.
Moving backwards or forwards controls their speed in the usual way, but
swinging sideways operates flaps on top of the wings called spoilers.
When a spoiler lifts up, the glider starts to turn to that side. These spoilers,
or in some cases even bigger flaps called 'ailerons' (which operate at the
trailing edges) mean that the rigids can turn with only a small amount of
effort from the pilot, rather like a normal light aircraft.

spars

ribs

A rigid's strength comes from the long carbon-fibre spars which form the fronts of the wings. The wing ribs which fit onto the spars are also made of carbon-fibre, which is very light and very strong – perfect for aircraft. The wing covering fits tightly, but can still be rolled up into a neat package for transport. The external framework is not as elaborate as that of traditional hang gliders, so there is less drag and they can glide more efficiently at up to 80 kilometres per hour.

As with hang gliders, there are training paragliders and competition ones, with many sports types in between. The gliders used at training schools are slow and stable. The canopies have about 20 or 30 large cells and don't collapse easily. At the other extreme, competition gliders may have 100 smaller cells. They glide very well and are fast but are hard to fly and can collapse rapidly in unskilled hands.

The pilot of a high-performance paraglider must be able to sense the air pressure inside the wing at all times. In rough air small movements of the brakes are constantly needed to stop collapses from starting.

The canopy of a training paraglider (shown here) is made up from a small number of large cells, giving stability and slow flight

A competition paraglider

Features that distinguish the competition paraglider from the training paraglider include:

- The competition glider's canopy is wider and thinner.

- There are many more cells in the canopy – up to 100 in total.

- The cells are smaller, which makes the canopy very sensitive.

- The lines are much thinner, which offers less wind resistance.

- The pilot can pull the front of the canopy down with a foot-operated bar for more speed.

- The harness is shaped in a slight curve and the pilot lies back to cut wind resistance.

Wing tip collapsing

Competition gliders are flown only by experts at top events such as World Championships. These professionals have had years of training and experience.

chapter 5: competition

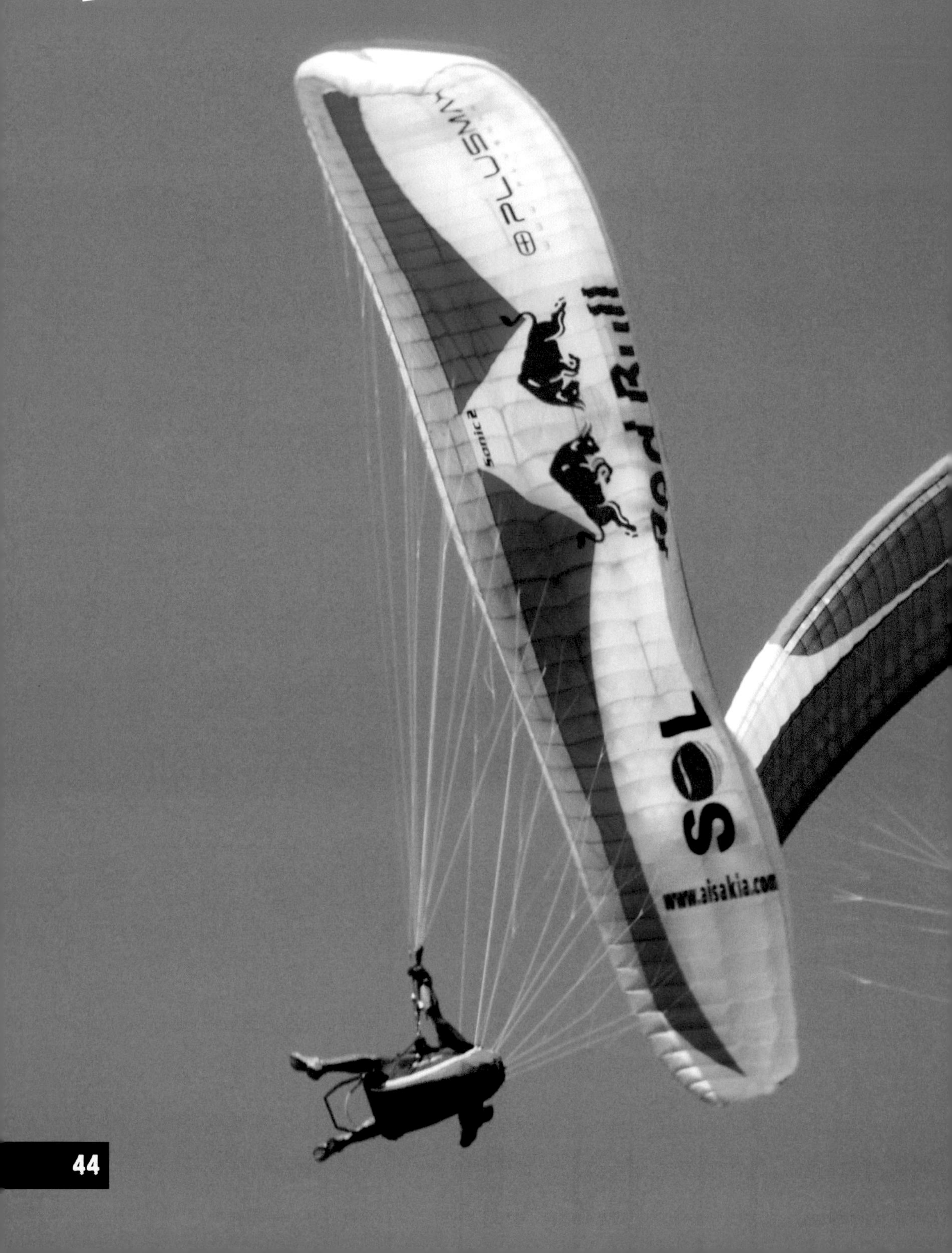

The competitors in a cross-country paragliding championship have about an hour to find good lift and gain height, before the clock starts for the timed part of the task. The goal they have to reach may be 70 or 80 kilometres away.

Competitions in both hang gliding and paragliding take place all over the world. Anyone can enter, and the starting age for competitors is 16.

There are several different types of contest for hang gliders and paragliders: cross-country racing (XC racing for short), landing accuracy (paragliders only), aerobatics – or Acro for short (mostly paragliders), speed flying and record breaking.

Hang gliders reach the inflatable finishing line after a speed race. These gliders can reach speeds of up to 88 kilometres per hour

Cross-country racing

This is the most popular type of competition for hang gliders and paragliders. A course is set by an expert on the local weather conditions. The course may be long — in fact, for hang gliders 160 kilometres is not uncommon. Start times are given and the competitors must record their flights on their GPS instruments. At the end of the day all the information about each competitor's flight, such as speed and height achieved, is downloaded from the GPSs to work out their overall position.

Paragliding accuracy competitions

In modern accuracy championships the pilots have to make a stand-up landing on a target. The pilots must stand up at least until the canopy touches the ground. Hitting the spot is much harder than it looks, especially if the wind isn't steady. The pilot has to watch the target and the windsock all the way down, while making tiny adjustments with the brakes. Pilots are penalised for each centimetre they land away from the centre.

Aerobatic (Acro) flying on hang gliders or paragliders is a very special skill. See an expert perform a loop and it looks easy and graceful, but if things go wrong, they can go very wrong indeed!

Acro competitions usually take place over a lake, with rescue boats at the ready. The biggest danger is that a pilot will fall into the canopy and become wrapped in it, unable to throw the rescue chute.

Pilots are scored for the difficulty of the things they do, and on how good the whole programme looks. There are both solo and pair classes.

Acro pilots can perform incredibly precise landings as part of their performance, like this one on a raft in the middle of a lake

Paragliders look spectacular doing violent turns and spins, their paths through the sky marked by smoke trails

Each manoeuvre has a special name, like Wing-over, Helicopter Spin, Titanic Manoeuvre or Infinity Tumble. Some are so difficult that only a few pilots in the world dare attempt them – they involve many loops and high-speed spirals. Acro canopies are extra strong to stand the hard use they get.

The first Acro World Championships were held near Montreux, Switzerland, in 2005. Huge crowds watched the colourful show from the lakeside.

Paragliding acro is far more popular than hang gliding acro, which is practised by approximately 100 people world-wide.

Othar Lawrence performing a wing-over, which is basically a 'slanted' loop over one side of the canopy

**Speed flying in
the French Alps**

Speed flying is the wildest of the free-flying sports. It is also the newest.
It is mainly a winter sport which takes place in mountain areas, such
as the Alps, in Europe. It combines off-piste and backcountry skiing with
high-level paragliding.

Speed flyers use very small, specially made paragliders and they wear skis.
The object is to skim down mountainsides just a few feet above the ground.
The canopies have to fly fast to make enough lift, so are usually launched by
pilots on skis who will sometimes touch-down and cross patches of snow on
the skis before zooming up to clear rocks. This is thrilling but very dangerous.
The canopies are small and very sensitive, so steering has to be precise.
If a pilot over- or understeers, they may crash into a mountian face. Another
danger lies in the speed — the top record for which is 146 kilometres per hour.

HANG GLIDING & PARAGLIDING

**Competition speed
flying down the Swiss Alps**

Hang gliders occasionally
fly similar downhill races
called Speed Gliding.

Speed Gliding competitions
are like a ski slalom in three
dimensions. The pilot
launches a glider from a
ramp, and races down the
mountain while passing
through 'altitude control
gates'. These gates are like
the flags in a slalom, but
the glider must pass
underneath them as well
as between them.

On top of that, there are the dangers from
backcountry skiing. The main one is avalanches
that could bury a pilot instantly in huge masses
of snow. It really is a sport for experts only!
Since January 2007, there are annual
championships that take place in Les Arcs,
in the French Alps. Competitors have to be
both very fast and extremely precise to win.

This involves flying and
diving at speeds of up to
130 kilometres per hour!
Although the winner of
these competitions is the
fastest pilot, competitors
also have to be very
accurate when they race
through the slalom.

All the official records for gliding are kept at the headquarters of the FAI (Fédération Aéronautique Internationale) in Switzerland. The FAI sets very strict rules which must be followed by anyone who wants to get a record listed.

Many competitions involve breaking records. There are three main types of record: distance and out-and-return distance, speed round a course, and gain-of-height.

Record breaking needs a lot of planning. The weather must be perfect for the task. An early start is needed for distance records, when the pilot must expect to be in the air for many hours. Out-and-return and triangle courses are difficult because there will usually be a head wind on part of the course.

Rob Whittall was the youngest person to be hang gliding World Champion at the age of 20 in 1989

Out-and-return A flight circuit that begin and ends at the same point and includes one turning point.

Course The distance between a start and a finish point, including any amount of turning points.

Austrian Manfred Ruhmer taking off at Seegrube in Innsbruck, Austria

Manfred Ruhmer from Austria flew just over 700 kilometres in Texas, for the Class 1 hang glider record in 2006.

The women's hang glider record is 402 kilometres, by Kari Castle of the USA.

The longest paraglider flight is by Will Gadd of Canada, at 423 kilometres.

When attempting height records, pilots take an oxygen supply, as the heights they rise to are oxygen-poor. The gain-of-height record for paragliders was set by Englishman Rob Whittall, flying in South Africa, in 1993. His gain was 14,849 feet – that's almost five kilometres, straight up! The gain-of-height record for hang gliders is 14,249 feet. It was set by the American Larry Tudor in California, USA, in 1985.

Two record holders: Kari Castle and Davis Straub; Davis holds the record for rigid hang gliders (Class 5) at 655 kilometres

chapter 6: people and places

Whether it's launching from the highest mountain in the world, or performing the most gravity-defying stunts, some pilots know no limits to making gliding sports even more extreme.

French couple Zeb Roche and Claire Bernier, the owners of an adventure sports school in France, set themselves the most adventurous task they could think of: to fly off the tops of the highest mountains in each of the seven continents of the world.

Zeb had climbed Mount Everest when he was only seventeen and was also a skilled paraglider pilot. Claire was already a paragliding champion, so they made a great team. However, it was still a huge task and took almost six years to complete. They set off in December 1996, using a two-seat paraglider and returned to their school after each successful conquest to raise money for the next challenge. The most difficult summit was Mount Vinson in Antarctica, which is very hard to get to.

Mount Vinson is located on Earth's coldest continent – temperatures can reach down to -90 °C in Antarctica

Tandem paraglider

Flying as a passenger in a two-seat paraglider – a tandem – can be a good way to experience free-flight for the first time. You will see advertisements for this service at many holiday resorts all year round. Zeb and Claire chose this method to paraglide from all the chosen mountain tops, as it was far more practical to only have to transport one paraglider up mountain sides.

Zeb Roche and Claire Bernier, Mount Everest

The journey to Antarctica depends on catching a flight from the southern most tip of Chile, and there were many delays due to bad weather. The highest launch was from Everest.

Asia	Mount Everest	8,850 m
South America	Cerro Aconcagua	6,959 m
North America	Mount McKinley	6,194 m
Africa	Mount Kilimanjaro	5,895 m
Europe	Mount Elbrus	5,642 m
Antarctica	Mount Vinson	4,892 m
Australia	Mount Kosciuszko	2,228 m

The acro kings

Felix and Raul Rodriguez started paragliding in Spain in their early teens. Now they are world stars of paragliding acro, famous for their solo and pair performances.

Mike Küng

Austrian Mike Küng is one of the boldest and most inventive pilots in the world. As well as performing loops – thought for years to be impossible on a paraglider – Mike has perfected ways of launching from helicopters and balloons. Mike also broke the height record in 2004, when he launched from a balloon at a height of 33,136.5 feet (4,118.9 feet higher than Mount Everest). The altitude meant that he needed an oxygen mask, and was covered in over an two centimetres of ice when launching!

Mike Küng launching himself out of a hot air balloon

John Heiney

American John Heiney was one of the pioneers of acro hang gliding in the early 1980s. He is a four-times Freestyle Hang Gliding Champion and holds the record for the most consecutive loops with a hang glider.
In 1988, John launched from a hot air balloon and managed to perform 52 loops in a row!

John Heiney performing a loop

Noel Whittall, the author of this book, and father of multiple gliding champion Rob Whittall, has been hang gliding since 1973. He designed and built his first hang glider from scratch! Here he answers some of the questions he is often asked.

Do birds ever fly near when you hang glide?

Yes, quite frequently. In fact, some birds of prey will attack hang glider wings, but it never gets dangerous. Birds also play an important role, because they seek out thermals. Spotting a soaring bird indicates a good lift to a pilot.

Noel with his second hang glider in 1974 – he built it from a kit!

What happens if the wind drops?

Nothing. Gliders fly at their own speed through the air regardless of the wind. It is called their airspeed. Of course, the wind does make a difference to a glider's speed over the ground. From the ground, a paraglider flying with an airspeed of over 30 km/h into a 30 km/h wind will seem to be standing still. If the glider turns and has the wind behind it, it will seem to be doing about 60 km/h, but its airspeed will still be only 30 km/h. Think about it...

The mountains in the Austrian Alps are up to 12,500 feet high!

What was the most scary situation for you in a hang glider?

I learned to hang glide in England, and all my flying was over low grassy slopes. Then I went to mountainous Austria with my glider. On my second flight, I found some good lift and managed to stay in it. For some time I paid more attention to my variometer than anything else. When I eventually did take a good look at my surroundings I was immediately hit by fear. I had just climbed above a whole mountain range! I was probably 12,000 feet high in the air. The sense of exposure was overwhelming as I clung on to the control bar for all I was worth. Although I knew I was on my usual glider which I trusted completely, it suddenly felt unstable, as if it would fall out of the sky if I moved a muscle. After what seemed an age I realised that I had to make myself take control, so I sped up and slowed down a few times, then flew a few circles, just to satisfy myself that I was in charge. Soon I was fairly relaxed again and enjoyed the rest of the 40 minute flight. But I'll never forget that first time high!

Glossary

Acro Short for Aerobatics; loops, spins, wing-overs and other aerial stunts performed with a paraglider.

Aerofoil The shape formed between the upper and lower surfaces of an aircraft wing to help the wing develop lift.

Ailerons Flaps fitted to the trailing edges of some hang gliders to make them turn in flight.

Altimeter Shows the height of the glider. Can be set to measure from take-off or from sea level.

Avalanche A very large and sudden rush of snow down a mountain that is seriously life-threatening to anyone in its way.

Backcountry skiing The backcountry is the entire area of a mountain outside resorts. Backcountry winter sports are extremely dangerous, as the terrain is unknown and the danger of avalanche activity is high.

Battens Stiffening ribs for hang glider wings.

Brakes Paraglider control lines.

Cells The individual divisions which make up a paraglider wing. Each cell has aerofoil-shaped fabric walls between the top and bottom surfaces, and an opening at the front to let air in as the wing moves forwards. The walls have quite large holes in them, so that the air pressure within the entire wing can remain fairly even when in flight.

Gliding The sport of unpowered flying that uses thermals and other forms of natural lift.

GPS Global Positioning by Satellite. An instrument very similar to the sat-nav units now found in many cars.

Joystick An aircraft control lever used on the Swift.

Leading edge Front edge of the glider wing.

Lift Rising air. Also used to describe the power generated by a wing moving through the air.

Microlight tug A small, very light aircraft with up to two seats that is used to launch gliders by towing them into the air.

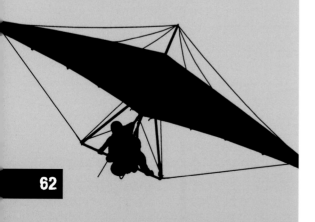

Off-piste skiing Pistes are regularly maintained slopes within a ski resort. Skiing off-piste means that the skier chooses a route that is not on the piste, but still within a resort. Resorts are regularly checked for potential avalanche activity, so they are the safe option for winter sport.

Ram-air effect The way a paraglider wing keeps its shape.

Risers The straps between the paraglider lines and the harness.

Rogallo Early hang glider. Named after Dr Francis Rogallo.

Rough air Air conditions that make it hard to fly, such as strong winds.

Sailplane A very light aircraft that is unpowered and flies with the help of thermals.

Sink Mass of air which is sinking. Gliders usually encounter them between thermals.

Slalom A race along a winding course marked by flags or poles.

Spoilers Flaps on the top of a wing which spoil the lift to make the glider turn.

Stall Sudden loss of lift caused by the air failing to flow smoothly over the wing. Usually caused by trying to fly too slowly.

Stockyard A large yard containing pens for livestock.

Trailing edge Rear edge of a glider wing.

Variometer This instrument shows whether a glider is climbing or sinking. It is essential for all gliders, because it is impossible to tell whether you are going up or down once you are a few hundred feet above the ground.

Wind-chill The apparent temperature felt on the skin due to a combination of air temperature and wind speed.

Windsock A light cylinder, usually made of fabric, attached to a mast. It shows the direction and strength of the wind and is often used on airfields.

XC Cross-country. If pilots say they are 'going XC' it means that they are not intending to land close to the launch site.

Index